## A New True Book

# THE VOYAGER SPACE PROBES

By Dennis B. Fradin

CHILDRENS PRESS ™

CHICAGO

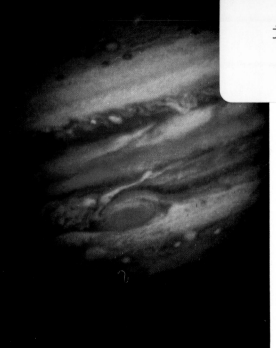

Jupiter

PHOTO CREDITS

Historical Pictures Service—9

Holiday Film Corporation—Cover, 2, 7 (top), 10, 15, 17, 25, 32 (3 photos), 34 (2 photos), 37 (2 photos), 41 (2 photos), 44

Jet Propulsion Laboratory, California Institute of Technology—29, 33, 39

NASA—7 (bottom), 13, 19, 23, 27, 31, 35, 40, 41, 42, 43

National Air and Space Museum, Smithsonian Institution—20

AP/Wide World—12 (2 photos)

John Forsberg—4, 5

Len Meents—6

COVER: Artist's concept of Voyager spacecraft passing Saturn

Library of Congress Cataloging in Publication Data

Fradin, Dennis B.
  The Voyager space probes.

  (A New true book)
  Includes index.
  Summary: Describes man's exploration of the solar system, with emphasis on the Voyager probes sent to the outer planets beyond the asteroid belt.
  1. Project Voyager—Juvenile literature.
[1. Project Voyager. 2. Outer space—Exploration]
I. Title.
TL789.8.U6V525  1985      919.9'04      84-23250
ISBN 0-516-01944-9          AACR2

# TABLE OF CONTENTS

# THE SOLAR SYSTEM

The sun and all objects that orbit it are known as the solar system. The sun, a yellow star, is by far the

largest object in the solar
system. Besides the sun
there are two main types
of objects in the solar
system—planets and
moons.

MERCURY

VENUS

EARTH

MARS

The planets are nine large objects orbiting the sun. The nine planets are Mercury, Venus, Earth, Mars, Jupiter, Saturn, Uranus, Neptune, and Pluto. Most of the planets are orbited by moons. Our Earth has one moon; several planets have many moons.

JUPITER

SATURN

URANUS

NEPTUNE

PLUTO

Saturn has rings and moons around it. Some of its moons are: Dione (in front), Tethys and Mimas (right), Enceladus and Rhea (left), Titan (top right).

Apollo XII photographed this "Earth-Rise" from its base on the moon.

# EYES AND TELESCOPES ON THE SOLAR SYSTEM

Once people had only their eyes to study the solar system. They saw Venus shining like a lantern. They watched the red planet Mars, giant Jupiter, and yellow Saturn. However, eyes were not strong enough to see details on those planets.

The first telescopes were built in the early 1600s.

Galileo (1564-1642)
built his own
telescope in 1609
and studied
the solar system.

With telescopes, people
could get closer looks at
the solar system. They saw
that Venus was white
because it was covered by

Mars

clouds. They saw green
markings on Mars, four
moons circling Jupiter, and
a ring around Saturn.
However, people still
wondered what those
objects would look like
from *very* close.

# EARLY EXPLORATIONS OF THE SOLAR SYSTEM

For years people could only imagine what it might be like to explore the solar system.

Then on October 4, 1957, the space age began when Russia launched an artificial satellite called *Sputnik I.* Soon Russia and the United States were using spacecraft to explore the solar system.

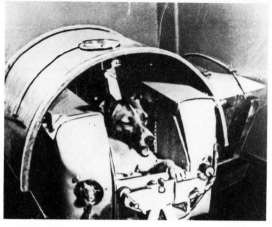

Laika (above) traveled in the bottom part of *Sputnik II* (left). The other parts carried instruments and radio transmitters. Laika died in space. There was no way to get her back to earth.

Both countries built space probes—unmanned craft that send back photographs and data to Earth. In 1959 Russia launched *Luna 2*, the first probe to land on the moon. That same year Russia's *Luna 3* was the

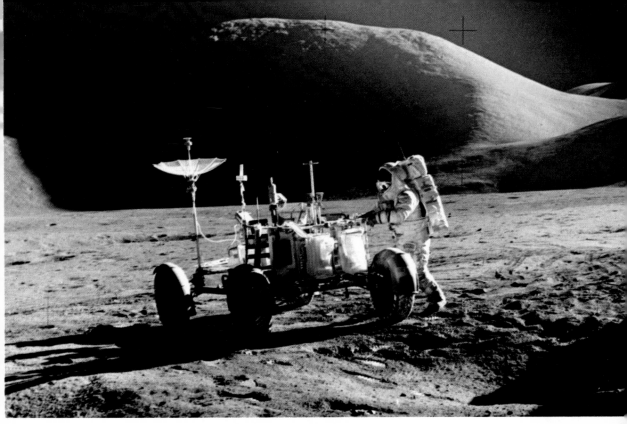

Astronauts explored the moon on foot and in the lunar rover.

first probe to photograph
the moon's hidden side.
The United States sent
probes to the moon, too,
and U.S. astronauts landed
on the moon six times
between 1969 and 1972.

Both the United States and Russia also sent probes to the planets. In 1970 Russia's *Venera 7* became the first probe to send data from Venus's surface. In 1975 the U.S. launched *Viking I* and *Viking II*, both of which took excellent photos of Mars. By the mid-1970s space probes had provided much data on Mercury, Venus, and Mars. Those three planets, along with

*Viking I* photograph of Mars

Earth, make up what are
called the inner planets.
But scientists still knew
little about what are called
the outer planets—Jupiter,
Saturn, Uranus, Neptune,
and Pluto.

# THE VOYAGER PROGRAM

In the early 1970s the U.S. launched *Pioneer X* and *Pioneer XI*. They sent back photographs and data on Jupiter and Saturn. Then the U.S. made plans to launch two probes to observe the outer planets in great detail. Called *Voyager 1* and *Voyager 2,* the probes were scheduled to be launched in the late summer of 1977.

*Pioneer 10* explores Jupiter

Scientists chose that time for a reason. They knew that during the late 1970s the outer planets would be lined up in a row. This event, which occurs every two hundred years or so, meant that the probes could zip from planet to planet without major changes in direction. The mission, nicknamed the "Grand Tour of the Outer Planets," called for the probes to pass near all of the outer planets except Pluto.

Two Voyagers were built because one probe couldn't provide all the pictures and data scientists wanted. Thousands of space workers spent more than four years building them. When finished, the

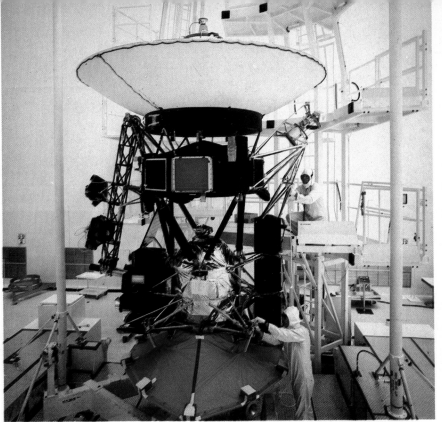

Test model
of the
*Voyager*
spacecraft

twin Voyagers were the
most complex unmanned
spacecraft built up to that
time. Each probe weighed
about two thousand
pounds. Each had many
instruments. Among the

Model of the *Voyager* on display at the National Air and Space Museum in Washington, D.C.

most important were the cameras that would send photographs to Earth. Other instruments would make infrared (heat) and radio studies of the outer solar system.

# BLAST-OFF!

The first Voyager was to be launched in late August of 1977. Although it would lift off first, it was called *Voyager 2*. This was because it would reach Jupiter and Saturn later than *Voyager 1*, which was to lift off in early September.

On August 20, 1977, thousands of people gathered at Cape Canaveral, Florida, to

watch the Titan-Centaur
rocket carry *Voyager 2*
into space. At 10:29 A.M.
Florida time, the voice on
the loudspeaker began the
final countdown:

"Ten, nine, eight, seven,
six, five, four, three, two,
one, zero!"

With a burst of flame
and a loud roar the Titan-
Centaur lifted off into the
blue Florida sky. Within an
hour, *Voyager 2* had
separated from the rocket

and had reached the speed of twenty thousand miles per hour. Within ten hours, *Voyager 2* was zooming past the moon on its way to Jupiter.

Sixteen days later, on the morning of September 5, 1977, *Voyager 1* blasted off from Cape Canaveral. *Voyager 1* was given a stronger boost into space by the Titan-Centaur. It

From eight million miles away *Voyager* photographed Jupiter and its moon, Io (in center).

headed toward Jupiter at a slightly higher speed than *Voyager 2.* That is why it would get there first—*if* everything went as planned.

# JUPITER AND SATURN

Day after day the two Voyagers sped deeper into space on their half-billion-mile trip to Jupiter. By November of 1977 *Voyager 2* had shot past Mars's orbit. In mid-December, as the probes entered the asteroid belt between Mars and Jupiter, *Voyager 1* passed *Voyager 2.*

The asteroid belt worried scientists. Asteroids are

In the future spacecraft might carry asteroids to orbiting space factories where they will be turned into things industry can use.

rocky objects that occur
mainly in a belt between
Mars and Jupiter. Would
the Voyagers pass safely
through this belt? Or
would asteroids destroy the
$320 million project? As

the Voyagers passed
unharmed through the
asteroid belt, everyone
involved in the project was
relieved.

In mid-1978 *Voyager 1*
began photographing
Jupiter. By December,
when it was still fifty
million miles from Jupiter,
*Voyager 1* was sending
back the best photos ever
taken of Jupiter. In early
1979, as *Voyager 1* closed
in on Jupiter, hundreds of

Dr. Laurence A. Soderblom explains the *Voyager* mission to newspaper reporters.

scientists gathered at the Jet Propulsion Laboratory in Pasadena, California, where the photos were being studied.

*Voyager 1*—and also *Voyager 2*, which arrived at Jupiter several months later—showed the largest planet to be covered by red, orange, gold, and blue clouds. Scientists had known that Jupiter is cloud covered. But they hadn't known about all the mighty storms that twist and swirl the clouds. Winds of up to 250 miles per hour were found on Jupiter.

Many other facts were learned about Jupiter. Flashes of lightning were seen in its atmosphere.

*Voyager 1* discovered that Jupiter had a ring around it.

Jupiter also was found to have a ring, like Saturn! Just twenty miles thick, this ring is made of tiny particles.

Other discoveries concerned the planet's many moons. The mission discovered several new moons of Jupiter, which

Europa

Callisto

Ganymede

has a total of at least
sixteen. The probes also
took close-up photographs
of Jupiter's four largest
moons—Europa, Callisto,
Ganymede, and Io. It was
learned that Europa is
almost as smooth as a
billiard ball, that Callisto is
covered by craters, and
that Ganymede has many

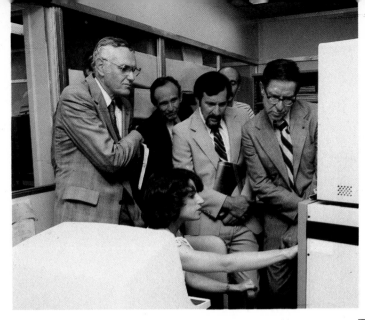

Linda Morabito, at
the computer screen,
was the first person
to find Io's
erupting volcano.

mountains and valleys. But
Io held the biggest surprise.

On March 9, 1979, Linda
Morabito, a scientist
working at the Jet
Propulsion Laboratory, was
studying a *Voyager 1*
photo of Io. She noticed a
bulge on Io's edge. It was
an erupting volcano! Linda

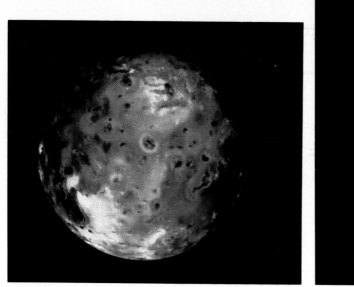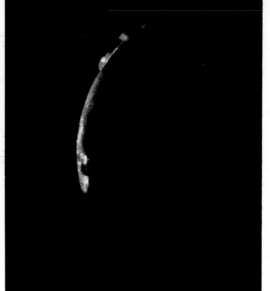

Io (left) and its volcanic eruptions (right).

Morabito had discovered
the first active volcano in
space. Later at least seven
more active volcanoes
were spotted on Io. The
dust and ash from Io's
volcanoes may have
provided the debris for
Jupiter's ring.

*Voyager 2* image of Saturn from thirteen million miles away

After Jupiter, the next
stop for the probes was
Saturn, one billion miles
from Earth. Even through a
small telescope, the
"ringed planet" looks
fantastic. Scientists could

hardly wait to see the pictures sent back by the Voyagers, which were to come within eighty thousand miles of Saturn.

In November of 1980 *Voyager 1* approached Saturn. Much was learned from this visit and from the one by *Voyager 2* in August of 1981.

Some of the biggest news concerned Saturn's rings. Saturn had long been thought to have three

These two images of Saturn (left) were taken a year apart by the *Voyager* space probes. Close-up of Saturn's rings (right).

main rings separated by large spaces. The Voyager photos showed that the planet has dozens of rings with few gaps between them. The rings were made of particles ranging in size from specks to house-sized rocks.

The Voyagers also revealed much about Saturn's moons. Titan's atmosphere was found to be mostly nitrogen, as is the case with our Earth. Several new moons of Saturn were spotted, raising the planet's total to more than twenty. It was also learned that many of Saturn's moons are composed mainly of ice.

Painting shows *Voyager 2* as it will appear when it approaches Uranus on January 24, 1986.

# URANUS AND NEPTUNE

After leaving Saturn, *Voyager 1* zoomed deeper into the solar system. *Voyager 2,* however, headed for Uranus and then Neptune. *Voyager 2*

Painting shows *Voyager 2* as it will appear when it passes Neptune and its moon Triton on August 24, 1989.

was scheduled to arrive near Uranus early in 1986. It was expected to reach far-off Neptune in 1989.

Meanwhile, astronomers are studying the information sent back by the Voyagers. They have 33,000 Jupiter photos,

Saturn's moons: Hyperion (left)
and Enceladus (above)

30,000 Saturn photos, and a mountain of information to study.

What formed the rings of Jupiter and Saturn? What causes Io's volcanoes? Perhaps the Voyager mission will answer these and other questions about Jupiter and Saturn.

# BEYOND THE
# SOLAR SYSTEM

By 1990, both Voyagers will be leaving the solar system. Perhaps, after thousands of years, living creatures will find the

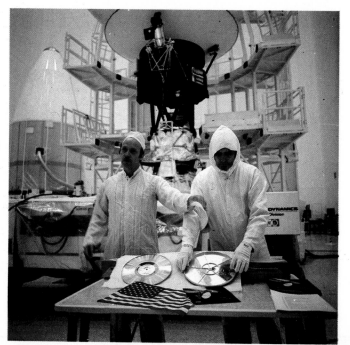

A *Sounds of Earth* record and an American flag were carried into space by the Voyager probes.

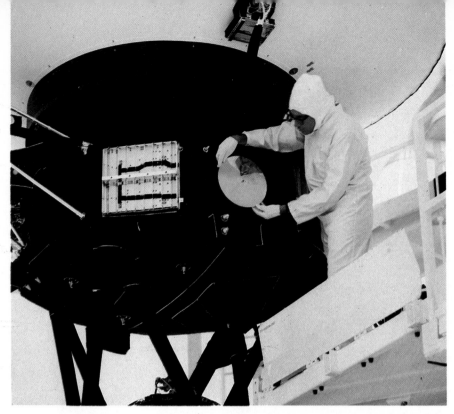

The record was carried outside Voyager.

Voyager probes. For that
reason, the two probes
carry messages from Earth.
A recording of music
and such sounds as wind,
rain, laughter, and
heartbeats was placed in

Artist's painting shows *Voyager 1* approaching Jupiter.

each probe. In addition, images of such scenes as a group of children, houses, animals, and the planets were placed in each craft. The two Voyagers have taught earthlings much about our solar system. Perhaps one day they will teach people on far-off worlds about us earthlings!

# WORDS YOU SHOULD KNOW

**artificial satellite**(ar•tih•FISH•il SAT•il•lite)—a man-made object that revolves around a heavenly body

**asteroids**(AST•er•oidz)—rocky objects located mainly between Mars and Jupiter

**astronauts**(AST•roh•nawts)—American space travelers

**astronomers**(ast•RON•ih•merz)—people who study stars, planets, and other heavenly bodies

**atmosphere**(AT•muss•feer)—the gaseous mass surrounding some heavenly bodies

**billion**(BILL•yun)—a thousand million (1,000,000,000)

**data**(DAY•ta)—information

**Earth**(ERTH)—the planet on which we live

**inner planets**(IN•er PLAN•its)—Mercury, Venus, Earth, and Mars

**million**(MILL•yun)—a thousand thousand (1,000,000)

**moon**(MOON)—a natural object that orbits a planet

**orbit**(OR•bit)—the path an object takes when it moves around another object

**outer planets**(OUT•er PLAN•its)—Jupiter, Saturn, Uranus, Neptune, and Pluto

**planet**(PLAN•it)—an object that orbits a star

**rocket**(ROCK•it)—a powerful engine used to propel a spacecraft; the vehicle propelled by a rocket engine is also called a rocket

**solar system**(SOH•ler SISS•tim)—the sun and all objects that orbit it

**space**(SPAYSS)—the region that begins about one hundred miles above Earth

**space probes**(SPAYSS PROHBZ)—devices that send back information from outer space

**star**(STAR)—a giant ball of hot, glowing gas

**sun**(SUN)—the star closest to Earth

**telescopes**(TEL•ih•skohpz)—instruments that make distant objects look closer

# INDEX

*About the Author*

*Dennis Fradin attended Northwestern University on a partial creative writing scholarship and graduated in 1967. He has published stories and articles in such places as* Ingenue, The Saturday Evening Post, Scholastic, Chicago, Oui, *and* National Humane Review. *His previous books include the Young People's Stories of Our States series for Childrens Press, and* Bad Luck Tony *for Prentice-Hall. In the True book series Dennis has written about astronomy, farming, comets, archaeology, movies, and the space lab. He is married and the father of three children.*